BETWEEN THE LINES

Volumes of Words Unspoken

Céline Zabad

ISBN: 1540422186
ISBN 13: 9781540422187
Library of Congress Control Number: 2017902492
CreateSpace Independent Publishing Platform
North Charleston, South Carolina

For my raison d'être: my parents.
To Rola, who pinpointed a "talent."
To Nizam, who hoped the talent would have to do with math or physics.
To both, who may be inevitably disappointed.

These aren't about you.
But they could be.

Table of Contents

UNSPOKEN

I crave a soul that vibes with mine,
A heart that beats my mind…
//A mind that reads the "me" between the line(s).

———

C-LINE

;

céline zabad

From my soul to ink on white,
To your heart, my way I'll write.
Till actions speak louder than my word—

Who knows…

I may just be able to change the world!

———

WORD

A world
within
a word.

———

LOVE

Elegance is an attitude,
   And I —
      Have an
        Attitude.

————

ELEGANCE

Morning sunshine,
Rays of today's warmth.

The wind dances
To the rhythm of my heart,
As it skips a beat—

With every flash of the past.

———

NOSTALGIA

;

céline zabad

Love
at its purest form
is unconditional.

UN-CONDITIONAL

Touch me in all the right places but one:

my heart.

————

DO NOT TOUCH

;

céline zabad

"You're a full stop; I, a comma.

You only know the end,
and I only know what follows.

The pain of trying to meet you halfway,
the reality of paths that will never cross…"

———

SEMICOLON

I am a run-on sentence.   Catch me if I can.

———

RUN-ON

;

céline zabad

Let's play tag.

@you'reit

———

@YOU

To be the *b* in doubt.

———

#SILENTMADNESS

;

céline zabad

The absent *u*
in my silhouette.

———

U

A tear dropped onto a piece of paper
and made love to the darkest of inks,

as letters soaked
and words drowned into silence.

———

WATER

;

céline zabad

Nestle me into your
parentheses.

I want to be your
amplified expression,
(*you*)r digression.

———

PARENTHESES

You are—

And so I am no longer.

———

EXISTENCE

Like autumn,
I ought to fall—
And die in colors that give you life.

———

FALL

The thing about good-byes, you see,
is the beautiful medley of a sense of loss
and self-discovery all at once.

Leaving all you know behind
to take that one step forward.

———

FORWARD THINKING

He loved Me.
I loved Him.

If only He were Him.

———

TRIANGULAR LOVE

He is the ink.

————

HE

;

céline zabad

Pleasure
And
Closure,

One thing's for *sure.*

———

CONCLUSION

Close-u-re
Close to her.
Close. Sure.
Closure.

———

LAST ACT

;

céline zabad

You left, and I don't even know what your favorite color is.

I never asked.

———

BLUE

I want to rip your heart out; then again,
I wouldn't want to stain my hands.

———

SULLIED SOULS

;

céline zabad

"You keep coming back;
I'm not even sure you ever left."
—Square One

"It's the dance, dearest,
where the beginning is the end
                    is the beginning."
—Round in Circles

―――――

FUTILE

He loved me so much,
he left.

———

TO LOVE AND LEAVE

;

céline zabad

You hugged me as if it were
the first time in a very long time...

As if it were the last.

———

ON A TRAIN

Ruffle my hair or fiddle with my heart…

Either way, you

        are

   like

      the

         wind.

———

INVISIBLE

3:00 a.m. thoughts

that never make it
as 3:00 p.m. words.

———

YOU

You are a figment of my imagination.
A fantasy, a fiction—
Based on a true story.

———

GENRE

;

céline zabad

There's always so much to be said
in between what was not
and what's in our head.

———

UNSAID

She wasn't the flame or the fire.

She was melted wax that dripped into you.

A hardened soul of teardrops that once were.

———

THE BLUE ZONE

;

céline zabad

In a match of you and me,
I am the back and forth.

Where I am Love—you are All.

A knotted tie of losers in a game for two.

———

TENNIS LOVE

Thoughts racing.
Who will make it first?

Pull the breaks.
The race has been reversed.

A wishful thought of a thought
that could have been a word.

———

COULD'VE

He walked all over me
like he was walking on eggshells…

And called it love.

———

CAUTIOUS LOVE

I don't want the number one,
a footnote in your research paper.

I want to be the main subject.

———

MAIN SUBJECT

;

céline zabad

And there's something about the rain…
The way the droplets kiss the earth,
The scent of wetness and damp dirt,
Like the lost art of handwritten love letters,
The forgotten forget-me-nots and faded, sealed kisses.

There's something about the rain…
The carefree way I used to dance with arms wide open to the heavens…
Tasting your every bit, drenching my very being…

I was younger then…

———

DRIZZLED FORGET-ME-NOTS

Her story within his
became history.

————

HIS-TORY

céline zabad

All things small—
Nothing like the small of your back.

———

SMALL

Isn't it wonderful…
The way a joey nestles into a
kangaroo's pouch,
How February's days fit perfectly
into a yearly calendar,
The way bases pair to create DNA,

How my palm fits in yours.

———

THE PERFECT FIT

;

céline zabad

Flying a kite reminds me of you...

How you held my hands back then
and guided me through,
How it pulls me now toward the direction of you.

———

KITE BEACH

I will contain you to the brim because I can.
Don't go for a swim just because you can.

———

OVERFLOW: TO GIVE AND BE TAKEN ADVANTAGE OF

Curiosity ran his fingers down my scar,
Turning a thirty-one-year-old story stitched with threads of then
into volumes of a now…
Chills ran down my spine, chasing a trail of sensations
gone in all directions.

———

ABOUT A SCAR

Marry my pieces, you have long ago, for your pieces are mine and mine yours…

I have disintegrated into a million hopeless pieces long ago, while no one was watching deliberately, and while my remnants float still, aimlessly, I remain the sole audience of this wreckage…

And that is OK…

Because when my pieces find their way toward one another, I will become whole. Alone. By myself.

And though I may think I am still the only audience of this union, you will have joined me to watch it all come together. Behind the scenes.

You have been the missing piece all along.

———

THE I WITHIN PIECES

;

céline zabad

You disrupt the sleeping patterns
of my hair follicles.

———

GOOSE BUMPS

He carried me like I was water—carefully.
Losing parts of me along the way.

———

SUM OF A WHOLE DIVIDED

;

céline zabad

Us

—A two-letter romance.

———

ONE

"I'm trying to kill time," he said.

Tic toc.
      —The sound of death by time for the nth time.

————

A LOSING GAME

He will be the end of her.

———

DEMISE

It is not in the hours in the days gone by
but rather in the seconds of spaces in
between that life happens.

———

IN THE BLINK OF AN EYE

The color of fear, wisdom, or age?
  Or is it the fear of aging or the
  aging that gave you wisdom?

Perhaps it's just the lack of melanin.

  It's a gray matter, I guess.

———

ANALYSIS OF A GRAY HAIR

He was an imam
    because he was godly.

Why they would name you after him beats me.

———

THE IRONY IN A NAME

She taught me that its sole purpose was not to carry water—that the perspective was not about half-full or half-empty.

A list of things to achieve or experience
    before dying—

But she,
    she taught me that it was about living.

———

THE BUCKET LIST

You're the dot to my *I*.
It's you at the end of my line.

A cool breeze caressed my skin in the scorching heat,
reminding me that you're here even though you're not.

———

MY I

;

céline zabad

I remember you in blues and a red,

The us that could have been,
    The you that lingers in my head…

———

BLUES 'N' RED

The best kind of friendships
are the ones that turn into family.

———

BY CHOICE

;

céline zabad

"Forever," he said.

Who knew that forever meant 143 days,
8 hours, 5 minutes, and 2 seconds.

———

FINITE FOREVER

Today is a better day.

When in your darkest hour, you realize the sun still shines outside for you.
When in all the chaos of your thoughts, a dear friend finds a way through.
When in the peak of your loneliness, the pen is there for you to hold,
To swing and sway to the rhythm of ink on paper and a story yet untold.
When in the heat of the moment, the wind caresses your mind with more of
what makes sense...
When the questions you screamed silently were answered but it was too loud
for you to hear the sound of patience...
When in the midst of all this misery, you realize that it's all about a state of
mind, then you've got loneliness redefined...

Today is a better day.

———

LONELINESS REDEFINED

;

céline zabad

...

You are my beginning and end…and all that is in between,
The break in my train of thoughts, the value in words unseen.
You are the one, two, three of an unfinished list, the echo of things left unsaid,
A pause—a loud silence of a dialogue lost in translation in my head.

The faltering, fragmented fiasco of feelings attempting to turn into speech,
The confusion and uncertainty that come in the form of an anticipatory breach.
You are the omission of invaluable words tangled within the rhetoric
Of you and me, an unfinished yet unstarted sentence destined to be poetic…

You are my unfinished thought, my slight pause, and my leading statement,
The mysterious echoing voice of my nervous and awkward silence, my abatement.

You are my "falling short," a clear conclusion that continues in sets of three.
You are what's missing to make me complete, but it's a given that you are my
reason to be…

My ellipsis
...

ELLIPSIS

"Breathe," he said.

How could she when he was the one
that took her breath away?

———

BREATHE

;

céline zabad

My heart just fluttered at the thought of you,
    All you passersby…
And I wondered what if…

Had you stayed for a while.

———

PASSERSBY

And she would go on to tell me
　　that the best kind of revenge
is to pray for the one who hurt you
　　and wish them well...

———

EXORCISM

There's something about sunsets
that makes good-byes
all the more worthwhile.

———

GOOD-BYES

"I'll be there for you," they all said…
They certainly were there—
Just not here,

Where it all really mattered.

———

SELECTIVE MORAL SUPPORT

;

céline zabad

Wish I could be a poet
So I can find the words to rhyme with *you*...

—or is it the other way 'round?

_____

CONFUSED WISHFUL THINKING

The scent of you on me
Lingers
Long after you've gone
  …
And nothing says, "Undress me,"
Like my skin
Wearing what's left of your cologne.

———

REMNANTS OF YOU

;

céline zabad

"Hello" is all that we seem to sing;
Listen closely; you'll hear a sort of silence ring…
"Good-bye" is all I hear—it's the only thing.

———

HELLO (THE END OF WHAT WAS)

I think of you all the time,
even when I'm not thinking of you…

————

I THINK; THEREFORE, YOU ARE

;

céline zabad

you and i:
different paths,
arm's length
distance apart,
side by side
moving as one,
divided,
searching,
yearning
to meet.
every move
made in unison, in
split synchronicity…

perhaps in another world,
a parallel universe,
our paths might cross.

but until then,
i try to count a blessing
instead of a loss.

———

PARALLEL LINES

I loved him.
Still
it was my definition of love

    that just wasn't enough.

––––––

IRRECONCILABLE DIFFERENCES

Behind those smiles are paragons of virtue and volumes of a love no heart can fathom—that's what happens when emotion meets passion.

———

SMILES

i feel
your presence

———

AT A LOSS FOR WORDS

It's the past tense that brings my demise.
It's the very same past tense that keeps me going.

———

HE LOVED ME

To think that he is the subject of my poetry is an inability to
move past the outlines of my words.

To get lost within the passion of letters side by side,
To sway with every curve,
flow with every line,
and complete the circle of every *I*,

To know what it takes to become a word wrapped
around another, only to transform into a thought that
beats to the rhythm of emotions...
To feel yet understand...
To be aware of all that, is to know that he is

merely the object...

———

THE CONTRADICTION IN DENIAL

;

céline zabad

Within the layers
　　of all that is her,
you'll find your
　　whole wide world…

But you're bound
　　to find home,
within the golden
　　hue of each
and every curl.

———

HER

You made that fire and set it to the bridge, annihilating every possible tie… yet you look me in the eye and tell me it was all because of the warmth I radiated.

You've tested my patience you've helped me practice.

But you taught me the greatest lesson of all: Being righteous with one who believes himself a saint is like mixing water with water.

I applaud you, though, on the audacity and the extent to which you believe your own lies.

It's been a great show; I'm just sick of the act.

I still have faith, because in the end, God will prevail.

———

YOUR TWISTED VERSION OF REALITY

Candlewick blue,
    Late night dinner for two,
    One of us doomed to be a fool…

———

FOOLING IN LOVE

In a sea of us, in the midst of chaos,
a Zabad:
the spume of whitecap waves.

In a sea of you,
in precedence to chaos—
what comes before,
what hugs the shore:
order—in a name and more.

In a sea of love,
in the midst of my heart—the essence of my soul is you:
Nizam.

————

ORDERLY CHAOS

I enjoy deep conversations, and somehow we always seem
to drown merely at the thought of one.

———————

STAYING AFLOAT

Home is where you are,
No matter the distance or time apart.
Seven are the deadly sins.
Seven is where mine begins.

To leave you behind
Is to separate heart from mind,
Take away sanity from what once was whole,
Replace it with subdued agony and a restless soul.

I love you so, my evergreen white.
It's been bittersweet to reunite
Only to bid you farewell once again
With no answer to the question, when?

You've been a father gained, a father lost,
A history unfolded, a tale embossed.
Hearts that beat as one—
Under the pouring rain of an African sun.

Circumstances seem to come at play,
But nothing can ever stand in our way.
Home is what I feel when I am with you.
Hold me close, and see me through.

No matter the distance or time apart,
My soul beats to the rhythm of your heart.

Home, my love, is where you are.

———

NIGERIA

And they say practice makes perfect, but that's rarely the case in matters of the heart and farewells…

And they wonder why I took so long to come back…

Who would've thought the second time would be more painful than the first?

When a good-bye feels like all the good-byes you've ever heard…

———

GOOD-BYES IN LOVE

I don't know how to travel light.

I come with a great deal of baggage.

———

BAGGAGE

To let go is to realize that all of this is actually a blessing disguised as a curse.

7:03 p.m. epiphany

———

LETTING GO

This world is but a fleeting moment…
Make the moments within the moment count.

———

LIFE

Homesick.

And not sure where home is.

———

THE WANDERER

Words

—a poet's compass.

———

NORTH

Silently and from afar,
The wish is still the same.
It's just a different star.

———

SAME BUT DIFFERENT

I see God in everyone, but the day I see
Him in you is the day my faith will
Have been tried and tested.

———

FINDING GOD EVEN IN YOU

;

céline zabad

What is rhythm without a rhyme
But a silent bell longing to chime…

———

ALL RHYTHM AND NO RHYME

"He loves me; he loves me not…"
—Death of a flower by a love that probably doesn't exist.

———

EFFEUILLER LA MARGUERITE

;

céline zabad

He loves you.
He loves you not.

Love yourself lots,
And just let him rot…

———

MARGUERITE'S RESPONSE

Follow me through, and
Let's part ways
...
Because even then, you
Shall follow me, too.

———

HAUNTING ADDICTION

;

céline zabad

The cling and clatter
Of a memory,
The ringing shatter
Of an unsaid "sorry"…

This clink and clank
Of chains of sorrow,
Of a today yearning,
Of a tired soul churning,
To turn a yesterday into a tomorrow.

———

GHOST OF THE PAST

And then there was poetry…

———

AFTER YOU

;

céline zabad

He said
she moved his world and turned it upside down,
she became the verb that turned him into a noun.

He said
she had his heart, perhaps in hers, but definitely in thrall,
she was the *S* he had been waiting for,
his be-all and end-all.

He said
he would go to the moon and back,
tread ground that no man had
to do, to be, to make, to have…

He said
he couldn't live without her.

He is now a father and married to another.

———

TRUE LOVE'S IRONY

"Once upon a time…"

How fairy tales begin *or* just a four-word story about what once was?

———

DOUBLE ENTENDRE

She loved me with a love I could not understand.

Before I knew it, all was lost within the quick of sand.

———

A CHANGE OF HEART

Red and a golden hue,
Colors of a kiss by you,

Burning fits of fever blush,
The aftermath of a heated touch.

———

SUN-KISSED SKIN

;

céline zabad

Follow my lead, for I
Have planted the seed.

In the end, there's no
Hiding plant from weed.

———

SEEDS AND WEEDS

We spoke poetry.
Now we speak silence.

———

FLUENT

;

céline zabad

He completed my sentences;
    he just couldn't complete me.

————

INCOMPLETE

She was the ink that kept running—
Only he abandoned the pen.

———

EXPEDIENCY

;

céline zabad

Reading you is like chasing the sunset
and catching the sunrise…

Only a select few capture both
within the beauty of a moonlit darkness.

———

IN LIGHT OF DARKNESS

With every whisper of wish and whoosh,
of water under burnt bridges—
are secrets solemnly sworn to be safe at sea…

———

ALLITERATION

Kiss me beyond my blushing point,
and let your golden hue and me be joined.

———

SUNBATHING

I once was a poet's muse,
    only now he prefers the blues.

Isn't it funny what we gain when we lose;
    sometimes love is but a cheeky ruse.

———

A RUSE AND BLUES

Just the way he looked at me was
in and of itself
a prayer.

———

ADORATION

Dip my soul in flowers, and shower me with a
love that flows like a river to the sea…

———

FLOW

;

céline zabad

Most make shrines out of human beings;
I would much rather build a home out of one.

———

WHEN HOME IS A PERSON

Just when you've started to get used to
the weight of the world on your shoulders, the weight of your
thoughts comes along and...

crash

_____

HEAVY

When you go out of your way for others, make sure you expect nothing in return, because sometimes nothing is all they can or are willing to offer.

—A lesson you learn the hard way.

———

EXPECTATIONS

There's something sad about an abandoned Ferris wheel...
perhaps it's the echo of youthful joy and carefree laughter...
or the endless clockwise rotation of life and the uncertainty
of a future that yearns to echo with the same youthful joy and
carefree laughter...

———

RAOUCHE FERRIS WHEEL

;

céline zabad

Where the sidewalk ends

Is where I will begin
To grow and mend
The path from within,
For it is only then
That the road not taken
                    Begins—
Where the sidewalk ends.

———

SILVERSTEIN FROST

And wherever those steps may lead me to,
I'll follow nature's colors beyond a shade of blue.

———————

STEPS

;

céline zabad

Do you remember when…
Do you remember how…

I just can't remember why…

———

THE WHY

Past, present, or future,

You were only a matter of time—

A tense.

———

PAST TENSE

;

céline zabad

It was a clear blue sky. The one that rests your tired eyes and
takes them on a stroll, only to glide through the fluff of a milky,
white cloud…

And what if those clouds were the spirits of loved ones passed?
What if they choose daylight over starry night to watch over us?

What if they are—our very own silver lining?

———

SILVER LINING

Woo me gently yet passionately,
With the magic of words ever so adamantly…
Resuscitate this dormant heart of mine.
Disrupt the rate of its normal resting line.

———

CARDIOPULMONARY RESUSCITATION

;

céline zabad

Often have I stolen moments of a cloud number nine,
Of happiness and so-called eternal bliss,
Yet I long for what's beyond and pine
Away on a cloud number ten and what went amiss...

———

CLOUD NUMBER TEN

The a.m. we often mistake for a p.m. is where it all comes from, the longing, the pain, the thoughts and voices…

Art.

Just art, in all of its forms.

———

THE ANTE POST MERIDIEM

He was a wordsmith, all right.

He played on words the same way he plucked and picked the
fretted strings of my heart.

———

GUITARIST

Twenty-six letters in the alphabet, and *I* am the only one that gets lost within *U*.

———

US

I:

Both a letter and a word referring to oneself…

To an existence that entails the complexity and sophistication of one's self…

———

I

Your love has burnt me into ashes.

You have inhaled my soul within yours only to exhale us both like dust in the wind...

And I wonder about the current state of your lungs...

———

CIGARETTE FLAMES

The competing sounds of a heartbeat and dial tone right
after the decision to part ways...

———

LOUD SILENCE

In a world of books, you are fiction, and I am the words that tell our story.

———

LIBRARIES AND LITERATURE

;

céline zabad

I often need your arms.

I yearn for a hug that will contain the skipping beat of my heart,
one that will restrain the madness of a creature gone
wild behind bars…

———

HAYWIRE HEART

Why put anyone on a pedestal when He's way up there and way
in here—within us.

In the end, we are only human, and
He's the creator...

———

IDOLIZING HUMANS

To those who fell in love with her voice
And those who fell in love with the song,
To those who fell in love with her writing
And those who fell in love with the poem,
To those who fell in love with her—
She is the song and the poem—she is art, and she will always be
the muse.

———

SHE

He used to write for her; now he only writes about her.
—A twelve-word story about a story that once was.

———

A WORD TURNED TWELVE

Why is it that we often fall in love?

Why can't we just fly in love?

———

TO FLY AND NOT FALL

You need me at your lowest; I want you at my best—
That's the difference between you and me.

————

DID YOU SPOT IT?

The weight of love is heavy.

———

BURDEN

Remember when…
When our love was on the rocks.

———

WHISKEY

If we know how it'll all end—our life, that is—do you think we would live in fear of what's ahead, or would we make the most out of every second until then?

———

LA FIN

When you fall apart, you'll find those who will walk all over your pieces, those who will search for them as if it were their life's mission, those who will try hard to put your pieces back together, and those who will take a piece or two for themselves…

And the best part of all of this is the front row seats you'll have while watching it all unfold, only for you to learn and let go of it all.

The best part is finding the pieces of your puzzle by creating new ones and putting them together all by yourself—because in the end, no one can help you if you don't help yourself.

———

PUZZLE

;

céline zabad

Murmurs of lost conversation in my head
Churn as I toss and turn restlessly in my bed.
Tic toc drawings of a perfect circle of time
As dawn conquers dusk and walks the line.
Sleepless nights into sleepless days—
As I wonder if ever you were mine…

Empty words I find in your somber pine;
You are now but a shadow in a drifting haze.

———

TWO YEARS AGO

Sacrifice (sa-krə-fĭs'):
A loss or something you give up,
usually for the sake of a better cause.

That's what the dictionary says.
I say,
sometimes it can be the greatest act of love.

———

ACT OF LOVE

;

céline zabad

Music mixed with lyrics of vodka and gin,
    Loud words amid a crowd silenced within,
    You lead the steps of a rumba in a coquetry,
Moving me to a rhythm of a word spree.

I soak the moment like a broken record,
    A love story recited in repeated echoes
    Rewinding my mind, pausing your moves.
Absorbing adrenaline, I slip into grooves,

Sunlit kisses upon my eyes the morning after
    A moonlit rumba of vodka lyrics and gin,
    Endless replay of meaning-ful-less chatter
Fading away with every heartbeat's chagrin.

———

THE DANCE

Let's get tangled.

———

KNOTTY

Crazy
In
Love
And
In
Pain.

No wonder it's a full moon.

———

SELENE

A gust of wind blew my way, picking up the pieces of all that was left behind.

Yellow leaves that once adorned the cold concrete asphalt now dance in midair chasing one another, through and through.

Time stood still.

In the midst of a loud conversation, the hustle and bustle of passersby, and the sound of metal on metal as the tram came to a stop—time stood still.

And so did I.

A rush of wind awakened my soul, reminding me that winter is coming. I could smell the taste of burnt coffee and feel the warmth of a steam telling of a summer gone by. But the chill of your absence became a story told through the aerial dance of autumn leaves.

You were gone, and that was OK, because even though winter was coming, summer was less than a year away.

———

EOLIAN SOUNDS AND PSITHURISM

Some people believe in love; others don't.
Some people think love doesn't exist, others that it is
                doomed or bound to fail…

I believe that love is a superpower we choose to hide; it is a
word we overuse, a feeling we undermine, a notion both under-
and overrated…

I say if only we stopped looking for it and instead became it—
Oh, what a wonderful world that would be!

    Love is here, but you, fellow human, have gotten used
    to destruction.

———

NOURISHING AND NURTURING LOVE

Love me like the wind loves a falling leaf in autumn…

———

THE FALL

White sheets,
  silky, messy,
    bare skin
      touching
        the light—
          rays shining through
      the windowpane,
        kissing a cheek,
          caressing a face

…

It's all going to be OK.

————

TODAY

Blah.

———

CURRENT MOOD

;

céline zabad

Lilac silk over soft skin left bare,
If you could feel it slip away...
Iron sinking, thinking deeply,
If you could fight for a breath of air...
Drums of sorrow, feats of feet,
If you could only race my heartbeat,

What would you do?

———

09.03.14

Perhaps the side effects (or withdrawal symptoms, as I'd like to call them) aren't so great because that's the price you have to pay for coming out of a state of pure nothingness, a state of not being, a loss of consciousness—peace.

———

ANESTHESIA

The trees have taught you the art of letting go.
    Take the fall then—
before the cold of winter gets the best of you.

———

WINTERIZE

Like ships in an orange sea of sky
Racing against the tic toc of our time,
Battling the sunset of you in me—

Don't sell me a story of us
That was merely built on a fortress of
      One too many a lie…

————

SHIPS AND CLOUDS

;

céline zabad

I find myself thinking of you on
   windowpanes and behind closed doors.

———

CLOSE

I know you prefer musical notes, my dear, but have you ever listened closely and carefully to the resonating sound of a

Word?

———

AUDIO FINGERPRINTS

;

céline zabad

In search of you,
    I traveled back in time
And found
    Home,
Without you.

———

TIME IS TELLING

Read into my actions and all that is in between

. . .

Only then should you watch the way I say the words

"I love you."

———

WHEN ACTIONS ENUNCIATE THE WORDS

I was your inspiration for that one season;
　　　　you were the inspiration that created my seasons.

————

MUSE

Love me, Tinder.
//A love song for this day and age.

———

ELVIS ROLLIN' IN HIS GRAVE

;

céline zabad

If you are the sea and I the shore,
How can it be that you long for me
But always leave me wanting more?

A sea with an 'S', a shore without sea,
Like chains and locks and only the one key,
A desire undefined and a pining mystery,

You come and go and quench and dry,
A droplet of you, and immersed am I.
The grain of grains, on a shore I lie

While your waves pull and hug,
As I get lost within the tug,
Washing upon me in the name of love.

Intimidation to admiration, you see,
Wishing your vim and valor if only upon me
Like a grain of sand that marvels helplessly at sea.

Afraid and shy am I, but not to swim,
For sometimes I join and go out on a limb,
Only to drown in a sea of him.

And each time that you must go
You're destined for other shores, you know…
Possibilities are countless where waters flow.
The promise remains only where the wind can blow.

———

THE SHORE AND THE SEA

There are emotions inside of me that words can't handle.

———

SPEECHLESS

They always come back…
 when it's too late.

————

RIGHT ON TIME

The overarching power of a notification.

———

LIKE, FOLLOW, COMMENT

My mind works at a speed of a million poems per you.

———

VELOCITY

Colors that paint the very thought of you.

———

RED

;

céline zabad

And then there are those who savor every comma and full stop, those who cannot hold their breath long enough at every pause, turning every semicolon into a doctrine, soaking in every word, taking in each letter whole and seeing it through its formation, creation, and enunciation—to thought, to feelings and words—to emotions and beyond.

There are those who not only read between the lines but also wander past eons of all that is me and focus on what matters…

They see my mind.

———

MIND OVER MATTER

Be thankful for what you have;
you don't have to have much to have everything...

———

MORNING PRAYER

;
céline zabad

Have you ever come to think just for a moment that perhaps her pessimism was a function of her fierce idealism?

That it was deeply rooted in and a result of all the disappointments the reality of life threw her way…

Think about that.

Just for a moment.

———

REALISM

Beyond the small, rounded airplane window was a sea of calm, serenity at its best. A painting of shades of metallic blue reflected upon a mirror of wrinkled water.

The very warmth of eyes twinkling against a dimpled smile.

Just for a moment, I was at peace.

Just for a moment, you were with me.

————

AIRBORNE

;

céline zabad

Words dressed in blue and black ink,
> Left bare within the eye of your
> Blink.

Eyes and words in total sync,
> As hearts lose all reason to
> Think.

BARE-NAKED WORDS

Love me like a comma holds a word from falling over, and I'll love you like a decorative sentence, a thought that is complete.

———

FULL STOP

Sway with me like ink on paper, writing my every curve with the tip of your mind.

———

THE WRITING DANCE

I see you in the waves, in shades of blue, in rays of me and you...

———

LIGHT

;

céline zabad

Stay.

—That moment when desire and pride come out to play and
you wonder which will have their way…

———

AMBIGUITY

Love me.

Oh, how often we say those words, just differently.

————

LOVE ME

Silence never felt so good.
Your thoughts, I hear them across oceans,
like thunderstorms raging to turn into words.

I hear them.
Loud and clear.

———

TELEPATHY

When mornings look like evenings
and thoughts of you are on repeat.

———

WINTER

Nothing that seems constant is here to say;
Many things come and go—few stay the same.
"Forever" is only a word at play.

Times change, and we with time. That's what they say.
Change is the only constant; that's the game,
Nothing that seems constant is here to say.

Like the fluff clouds still, slowly moving away,
Or a burning fire that was but a flame,
A sun that sets—at dawn comes out to play.

A night so young bound to turn into day,
Memories captured and kept in a frame,
Nothing that seems constant is here to say.

Leaves of fall to the greens of spring and May,
All that's left of who you were is a name,
Flowers to petals of hearts on display.

You'd speak to me in poetry today,
But a songwriter for her you became.
Nothing that seems constant is here to say;
"Forever" is only a word at play.

———

A WORD AT PLAY

It ended before it began.
//The shortest love story ever—even shorter than
Ernest Hemingway's six-word short story.

———

FIVE-WORD SHORT STORY

céline zabad

We were never the same distance apart—a story of two lines that never intersect, meet, or touch at any point…

I did the math…

…And, my, did we get so close; we almost touched.

//Almost to infinity and beyond with a distance that tends to zero.

———

ASYMPTOTES

I miss you like a page misses the next,
    like February misses twenty-nine,
like the moon misses the sun—

    every single time...

//You are missing from me.

———

TU ME MANQUES

;

céline zabad

2:00 a.m. spells of sadness,
ill-founded melancholia,
ruminating…
the mind won't stop
with the deafening chatter,
keeping my heart wired
with anxiety,
pumping life into me,
as I lay my head restlessly
on a pillow
that has often kissed my salty cheeks
good night.

only it was morning,
and even though the sun had yet to rise,
I had a playground all to myself,

a mood swing
to ride
and ricochet
between
high and low.

MOOD SWING

How can I write of love and loss
When I am at a loss for words,
And you are love?

————

THE ONLY WORD

;

céline zabad

The insurmountable beauty
Of a lack of leaves and nudity,
The death within a life
Of a winter's dormancy,

A bare melody, a moving eulogy,
You are a different kind of poetry.

————

POE-TREE

You are slowly fading away…
like a sweet morning perfume,

scent on skin
touching
salient senses
with a strength to travel far
long after it has left a mark
etched in olfactory systems,
stripping away all forms of resistance

as I madly question my existence.

———

EVANESCENCE

;

céline zabad

Can you see what's in store for you and me in this Turkish coffee cup of a blue sky? Mysteries and fortunes and come what may—but it certainly all doesn't matter, for all I see is you finding your way through the darkest of clouds to me.

———

CREPUSCULAR RAYS

The moon would stay up every night waiting for the sun to rise, only to witness the colors of passion and ardor mesh with cold waters in an intimacy that made even the blue sky blush away...

Her sadness grew heavy, her envy strong, that every now and then she would do all that she could to pull the waters away, away from her beloved sun.

While she fell victim to a triangular love of circular motion, there were billions falling in love with her light every night as the sky would roll out a carpet of constellations in her honor.

Let the sun set, my love, so you can shine on for true lovers of the night!

———

HIGH TIDE

It skipped a beat.

Ever since then, the rhythm was never the same again.

———

UNCHAINED MELODY

Tame me.
//The fastest way to lose me.

————

SHREW

;

céline zabad

---

in
lost
with
you

———

PARAPHRASE

The only things jingling this December
are my love handles.

————

BÛCHE DE NOËL

Thinking of you thinking of me.

———

THE THINKER

Those who don't believe in soul mates probably haven't met theirs yet.

———

NONBELIEVER

;

céline zabad

Only now do I understand why silence is the best response; because some insecurities can be loud—

In fact they can be deafening.

———

...

She was made with needles, sewn with
fine threads of dark and bright colors, woven with love and
thoughts that have come and gone to ocean depths…Every thread
stroke told a story embroidered with imagination, stitched into an
existence that could read the touch of your skin, feel the scent of
your pores like a lazy Sunday afternoon when the coffee had gone
cold and her lipstick stains were telling of a brighter future than
what the cup foretold.

She now weaves and knits and knots
herself into your sidelines, tailoring away silent words inside out, all
the while bursting at the seams of your hem, attempting to bring
the fibers of all that she is into the fabric of all that you are. It was a
pattern, you see, and all she had to protect herself from the pain was
a thimble. But that was OK, because at the end of the day, the story
was created by her and her alone: the end knot at the back of it all.

And she wore it gracefully.

———

COMPLICATED

;

céline zabad

---

like
   a
tired
   soul
misses
   sleep

———

RESTLESS

You want me to set into the sea and make way for your reflection
across waters, forgetting that against a waterfall backdrop, you and
I and the sea become one.

Relentless in your pursuit while I
burn endlessly for you...

It is what it is—short-lived moments of total bliss, of a
bittersweet and rare kind of solar eclipse.

———

SELENE AND THE SUN AS ONE

No man will ever be more important than you.
My love life is one thing, but my life, you gave it to me.

You are my reason to be.
//My father.

————

RAISON D'ÊTRE

Will you kiss me under the mistletoe
In the cold of winter and the white of snow?
Will you get lost in the red of cheeks and lips
And hearts tangled in a skip within grips?

Will you kiss me under the mistletoe
And get tied up in the mess of a perfect bow...

———

TIES AND TRADITIONS

;

céline zabad

what if the stars were watching us
and wishing upon a you and me
                burning, falling in the name of love
because all along we were the ones—

we were their sky…

———

STARDUST AND A DIFFERENT PERSPECTIVE

Our heart—it's soft and fragile and behind a
rib cage for a reason...
    It pumps warmth and love and life...
        It was made to love—beyond reason—
It is the very reason we are human.

        Tell me then, how is it that we are capable of so
much destruction?

————

REASON WITH ME

;

céline zabad

We don't talk anymore.
I'm here, and you're there;
We've both closed that door.

Only it's unlocked…

———

CLOSURE

You

My
    Sin-
        Dro-

Me

The symptom and the last word.

———

SYNDROME

;

céline zabad

My heart—

It is heavy with the intangible.

—————

YOU

He fell in love with my words
And I with his soul…

It was all the same language,
Just a different dialect…

———

LINGUISTICS

When the moon is half-out trying to catch the sun with a full heart.

———

HIDE-AND-SEEK

The way he said my name—

Even time had to take a minute and
soak in a silence that had never been so loud.

————

MUSIC

Hold me.

//The way the sky cradles the clouds.

———

ANALOGIES

The branches of bare trees,
The life within a cold breeze,
        The birds and bees and living things,
The kindred spirits of human beings,
    The light of a burning sun…
            I see you in all of it—

No wonder you encompass the number
One.

———

THEOPHANY

;

céline zabad

the stillness of those clouds,
bright lights shining through.
the stillness of my heart,
racing beats to motions of you.

violins and hearts at play,
strings attached at bay...

————

NO STRINGS ATTACHED

It was never
    Me.

It was only ever
    The idea of
        Me.

———————

THE IDEA

;

céline zabad

Miss-drawal symptoms

———

WITHDRAWAL

Kiss my constellations to sleep,
Caress those scars that quietly weep,

Till skin on skin turns to dust
And fate connects the dots of us.

———

BEAUTY MARKS

There's no reproach in love.

There's your approach—
and that, my dear, makes all the difference.

———

THIS ONE'S ABOUT YOU I

Changing your principles for someone is not love.

It's just weakness.

———

THIS ONE'S ABOUT YOU II

I can't read your lips. Could you rewrite all over mine?

———

LEGIBILITY

It takes two to tango,
But I'd rather dance as one.

———

INTIMACY

;
céline zabad

You got inside my head.

You seeped through
the syllables of every word, reading between fine lines of
wrinkles and soul prints. Tell me, was it dark enough? They
say a mind like mine is a terrible place, with sharp thoughts
and profound expressions. Did you find you in every corner
of me? Could you figure out the way through the labyrinth and
inner workings of a machine tirelessly churning at the thought
of you? Did you get your skin soaked in ink? Did you find the
words I often get lost within?

You got inside my head.
//You were the last word I ever read.

———

INSIDE MY MIND

She may be the song you long to sing,
The poem of words stained in ink.
                She may be the breath she took away,
    The meaning behind the words you say.
She may be the sun and the moon,
                The reason behind your fall into a swoon…
    She may be the love of your life bar none,
    The apple of your eye…
All I'm trying to say is

I could be the one.
    //She is not me.

———

1.1.17

To be
Thought-
Ful,
In a world of
Thought-
less
Is a pain-
ful less-
on.

———

SUFFIXES

It is the first page of 365 days, but it's also a continuation of a story that's been in the making for as long as you can remember.

//Evolution of story and characters.

————

TO BE CONTINUED

;

céline zabad

"You're too sensitive," he said—
like it was a bad thing.

———

OFFSETTING YOU

Perhaps we dream because we long for those on the other side of this world…

And perhaps we have nightmares because those who love us here and now are longing to be heard.

————

WHAT DREAMS MAY COME

;

céline zabad

And so you looked for me in another
And found that there was no other…

———

TOLD YOU SO

A loud silence
Of howling oceans,

A bittersweet
Rollercoaster of emotions

Of the beginning of an end,
Of a sea of grief,

A painful sigh of relief.

———

PARADOX AND METAPHORS

Hug(e)

———

SNUG

I was never really yours to love.
You were just in love with a word:
"mine."

———

BELONGINGS

I want to love and be loved deeply, passionately and beyond reason, but the confines of reason were made for the heart in fear of losing her.

//She wants to get lost.

———

THE REASON BEHIND REASON

If rib cages were made to tame those wild creatures we call hearts, then why is it that hearts often skip, fall, or find home in the hands of others?

———

WILD CREATURES

Reason loves a heart that yearns to love
what is beyond…
    Where he reasons with her, she
flirts with others.

———

REASONING WITH EMOTIONS

He wanted her to be sensual,
So she went ahead and
touched his soul.

———

RETICENCE

;

céline zabad

...

//Those three little words.

———

IDIOMS

Entertain and fuel those notions.
Strip me of those emotions.

————

BARE

;

céline zabad

When "love" becomes synonymous with "leave"
And the meaning of words becomes hard to conceive,
When a vowel is replaced with two
And all that's left is *I* and *U*.

//a, e, i, o, u

———

VOWELS

Tattoo your kisses on my skin;
Smudge those words with your fingertips.

———

INK

You know when you look up at the sky and the sun caresses your face, kissing every corner, smoothing over every rough edge, and breathing in your pores…You know how the rays land on your eyelashes, glistening timidly, making you blink like a heart that skips a beat or two as you try to capture the beauty of what's looking straight at you…You know that feeling of just the right kind of warmth, the perfect touch that moves you just enough to know you're at peace, even if it was just for a few seconds?

Yes…

That feeling.

———

GOLDEN

Wrapped around your finger,
I've got you
Wrapped around my heart.

———

WRAPPING ROLLS

;

céline zabad

People often listen with the intent to reply, when the only response needed sometimes is silence and an open heart.

———

ALL EARS

As an idealist, no one will ever exceed your expectations, let alone meet them.

IDEAL REALIST

;
céline zabad

There's something about this hour,

        the in-betweens
    of a world at peace,
        breathing in the last of dreams
within the deep of sleep,

as I am fully awake,
        thinking, listening, and
        counting sheep.

———

5:00 A.M.

I have often wondered why you carried a lighter and why you would light a match only to burn what kept us near.

I have often been saddened by the loss of love, the idea of us becoming strangers after having surpassed every boundary of the word.

I have often been that someone.

This year I will also watch you light up things, only I will sit back, relax, and watch the beauty of destruction in the making: ties severed and bridges burned. In other words, freedom and light.

Oh, and a very warm heart.
//On burning bridges, volume 2017.

————

BLAZE

;
céline zabad

We both wanted a place to hide,
    So we found comfort in each other's hearts.

    We both wanted a world different than ours,
So we sought imagination in each other's minds.

———

SANCTUARY

Winter cold.
Hot showers
   Of steam
Rinsing off
Today and yesterday.
   Counting my blessings,
I gasp,
   Catching a breath of a life
      I had lost.

Pangs of agony,
   Goose bumps of melancholy,
Well up in a moment's paralysis,

Reminding me of a loss
I might have forgot
   While counting
      One-too-many a blessing
Lost within a single loss.

//When a loss drowns all your blessings.

———

ACUTE PAIN

;

céline zabad

Whisper closer.
Move me with your words.
Lip-synch my senses into a blur,
And let your breath blow kisses of free verse
Against nape and neck yearning to converse.

———

FRISSON

You send chills down my spine
That have the hots for crossing every line.

———

RED LIGHTS

;
céline zabad

The sweetness in a complication
That gets you in a sticky situation.

———

HONEY

Like the ends of a cigarette,
          Home was your lips, and you drawing me in
          meant the death of me.

———

IN FLAMES

;

céline zabad

I love it when you put me in a corner—
Back against the wall,
and everything else is up against you.

———

TIGHT CORNERS

The power of words
                    Spoken with
        The eyes.

———

MEDIUM

;

céline zabad

Run your fingers down the gold of my skin
And read those scars
Like the silver lining
That they are.

———

BRAILLE

They call it falling in love
because every so often,
you're catching your breath.

———

THE FALL AND CATCH

;
céline zabad

To cut me off in the middle of a conversation with
a loss for words and a sigh…
For whatever is left is said with our eyes.

———

CONTACT AND CONVERSATIONS

Hearing you breathing on the other end of the line
is a melody of a sweeter kind.

———

SILENT PHONE CONVERSATIONS

;
céline zabad

I've given away too many pieces of my heart
To have any peace of mind left...

———

BITS AND PIECES

Her mother tongue was
his body language.

————

FLUENT

;

céline zabad

Free falling,
    Falling into trouble,
        Falling in love,
           And falling into you:
Merely synonyms of a sinking heart.

———

THE FEELING BEHIND FALLING

Nigeria,

the heart of Africa,
the whole of my heart.

———

HOME

;
céline zabad

It ain't the kiss nor the lips,
But rather the hugs and the grips.

———

EXPRESSIONS

I am one of those who will often walk head
    down, comfortably lost in my own thoughts, but
when the darkness comes, I always look up in search of you.

You asked me once to describe what it was like—
how could I, when it's your soul that's shattered into a
    million and one luminous twinkles,
                    shining so bright over me,
making me feel tiny enough yet protected by the vast blanket of
your embrace?

        A million and one scattered pieces of your soul,
like fairy dust in a moonless sky—you are all, a constellation, a
galaxy, and I am that one piece looking up, a reflection, a mirror
of all that I see…

all that is you.

———

STARRY NIGHT

;

céline zabad

It is what it is.
Neither that nor this.

———

STATUS QUO

Most of us know what it's like to have a
complete stranger
  become the closest
  thing to you, and most of us also know
  how sad it is to have the closest thing to
  you become a
complete stranger.

  It's like knowing your favorite book by
  heart, only you can't read the words
  you've become so familiar with.

  ———

  STRANGELY SAD

;

céline zabad

I was always the "so" in "whatsoever," never
the "what" nor the "for" in "forever."

//Caught in the middle, cutting a whole
into one three many a syllable.

———

TMESIS

Sometimes convenience makes
what is beyond our control
quite controllable.

———

BEYOND MY CONTROL

And then I realized I wasn't made for everybody…

And that was the crux of my tragedy—
Or theirs.

———

TRAGEDY

Have you ever seen two waves collide and crash on a sandbank?

It's like lovers quenching each other's thirst after a lifetime of searching for one another only to be separated again, knowing that when the time is right, they will hug at shore once more and let their souls collide forever more.

————

SOUL BANK

;
céline zabad

Stop singing that same old song,
   and write some poetry about

how you did me wrong.

———

ATTEMPT AT AN APOLOGY

Take me away, and color my soul
with the rainbow of your touch.

———

PARASAILING

Get to know me like you love me.

//Ask me questions, and then ask me some more. Show me that you're curious, that you're intrigued, that you have a thirst for all that is me. Beat me at my game, because you already know before even knowing that I'm the kind of person who would be curious enough to ask all the right questions—to know you like I love you, to love you like I already know all the questions that make you tick and all the answers that would make us click.

———

LOVE AND CURIOUS QUESTIONS

I am broken into a million little pieces.

I am words crumbled into letters…

And I can't muster up the strength to put "me"
back together again.

Let me be like a dandelion dispersed into the peace
of nothingness…

———

LEAVE ME BE

;

céline zabad

A pensive mind,
    A racing heart,
A troubled soul.
    The weight of a body
Everyone should condole.

———

TIRED

My story revolved around him:

The ink and meter,

The prayer and hymn.

———

HOMONYMS

;
céline zabad

And then you made me feel.
//All else was forgotten.

———

LOGIC

I can't remember the last time I forgot about you.

———

RECOLLECTION

You set so beautifully;
Take me with you ever so gracefully.

———

LIGHT

Her heart kept shielding itself from
within until she grew the thickest of skin.

————

WHEN SHEEP TURN INTO WOLVES—RELUCTANTLY

;

céline zabad

We talk about love and think chemistry and
biology, when in fact it's all physics:

forces and motion,
momentum and energy,
heat and light,
electricity and magnetism…

//The physical properties and phenomena of you.

———

PHYSICS

I don't want to be the only one. I just don't want to be one of them...

———

DIFFERENT

;
céline zabad

Don't be fooled by her small hands;
They've carried the weight of the world.
//And you.

———

BIG HEART

A memory in passing lost,
  Rekindled in
    A union in passing gained.
      //Things happen for a reason.

————

SERENDIPITY

;

céline zabad

Let's play

hide-and-seek

in your

kiss and hug.

———

GETTING LOST

I wish I could explode into a thousand rays of light and show you what love is made of and all the magic I am capable of.

———

A TOUCH

;

céline zabad

Love,
    Underrated
        And
            Overrated.

CONTROVERSIAL

That moment when your eyes lock only to look away swiftly and timidly,

Because you got lost merely at the depths of a soul's surface.

———

IN LOST

You had to lose me to find you,

When I lost myself within you.

———

FOUND AND LOST

Doses of dopamine and serotonin,
Colliding cuddles of oxytocin,

You encompass every endorphin,
A chemical warfare of epic proportions.

———

THE SCIENCE OF LOVE

They all were "one of a kind" in your eyes at one point in time, only now it's time.

//Taking turns.

———

MY TURN

It is the darkness of her brown eyes that is very
telling...

———

INVISIBLE TEARS

;

céline zabad

I saw a clown sell cotton candy on the side of the street, and it
made me think how sadness can be so giving...

———

COMIC RELIEF

It's funny what you lose when you're lost.

//The art of…

———

LOSING

;

céline zabad

I live in the same house
I lost you in.
//What a realization.

————

UNBEARABLE

She constantly felt the need
to tell him how much he meant to her…Maybe because she was
too familiar with loss.

———

JUST IN CASE

;

céline zabad

I'm sorry I stripped my heart naked for you—

I thought you could handle it.

———

THINK AGAIN

Darling, but they loved you not for who you are
But for how you make them feel.

//When the concept is misunderstood.

———

CONDITIONAL

;

céline zabad

We logophiles are so in love with words that we often get carried away and end up saying way too much.

//More than we should.

———

SILENCE IS GOLD

Chilled glass of wine,

Red

Lipstick stains

Melt

With every drop of

Sweat.

———

CONDENSATION

;

céline zabad

People don't see their mistakes.

They only have eyes for yours

...

So make it scenic.

———

HUMAN

Turning feelings into words.

————

QUANTUM ENERGY TELEPORTATION

;

céline zabad

M–ss–y

When the vowels are missing, you can't breathe.
When the consonants are there, it's a tease.
Where one is about your vocal tract and lungs,
The other is all about the lips and tongue.

———

I MISS YOU

I watch the moon
While you wake up to the sun.

    I am awake dreaming of you
    Sleeping in a different time zone.

But love, my love comes in different forms
And fails to comprehend the concept of

    You and me
    As one.

———

TIME ZONES

;
céline zabad

Silence is the best storyteller.

———

VOLUMES

Missing you is like forgetting one's name.

————

PAINFUL

Heart:

    Love me;

    Hug me;

    Want me;

    Need me.

Brain:

    You're enough on your own to give all of that to yourself.

———

REASON

The best way to be misunderstood is to care too much.

———

ADVICE

;

céline zabad

Your love is too sweet;
your heart must be an icky place.

———

SWEET TALK

Let's go back to what we were

before we became what we are.

———

REDUNDANT

I can see the future, but you call me crazy
because you live in the present.

//The power of now versus the future.

———

SIXTH SENSE

Boughs of you laden with me,

An arrow to his bow so quick to set me free.

———

HOMONYMS II

A heartbreak is but a break from the familiar,
And yours was merely a skip to a different beat.

———

BREAKING HABITS

She could not stay.

She was like the seasons, forever changing…only to return once again in a cycle of come what may.

———

EVER CHANGING

;

céline zabad

Holding on to loose strings, and the only thing pulling me back to reality is gravity…

//The weight of things.

———

SOLO

You can't understand her mind and know her heart yet
ridicule her thoughts and question her love.
//What she is made of.

————

CONFUSING

;

céline zabad

You need to see yourself the way I see you—
through my eyes. For only then will objects in the mirror appear
as they are—

a reflection of all things love.

———

LOOKING GLASS

I look at lakes and often wonder what lies beneath the silence...

———

DEPTH

;

céline zabad

How do you tell loved-one-turned-strangers
you miss them?

———

MISSING THE POINT

I love bare trees because I see beauty
before it blooms.

———

UNCONDITIONAL SPRING

;

céline zabad

Eventually,

it all fades.

———

EVERLASTING

All it takes is a couple of layers to find out the fate of infatuation…

———

UNRAVELING

;

céline zabad

They want me to open up, but then they judge my words.

———

FAIR

"You can't take a compliment," he said.

Well, you know my name and face, but did you study the edges of my soul? Have you found your way through the dusty corners of my mind? Did you count the freckles on my skin and figure out the meaning of my sign? And when my eyes look at you, what do you see? Do you know the different curves of my smile or angles of my thoughts? Did you attempt to find out the answers to questions you are craving to ask, only to go through the labyrinth of me and come out in more awe than you went in? Did you do all that and then choose to compliment me? Because only then will I know your words are here to stay…

Only then will you find beauty in the way I take a compliment.

———

GENUINE

;

céline zabad

The problem with being impulsive is that you might regret even
the nice things you do or say.

//Intentions aren't for everyone.

———

I'M PULSE

You often find solace in the unexpected when the expected is a disappointment.

———

SERIES OF UNFORTUNATE EVENTS

When you become fluent in my silence as a language, only then

will you have the ability to comprehend my words.

———

ELOQUENCE

Soul

    On

Soul

———

MAGNETIC RESONANCE IMAGING

;

céline zabad

As
I
Lay down my head,
my

heart

is heavy with

you.

————

PILLOW TALK

You came into my life,
    Made a mess,
And left.

...

And they wonder why they name

Hurricanes and storms after people.

———

METEOROLOGY

;

céline zabad

You hurt me with the sharp edges of your words till they became dull…

———

KNIVES

Arms locked around his neck,
    Arms locked around her waist,

Chest on chest, whispers of a peck,
    Heart to heart craving an embrace.

———

SNUG HUG

Many call you a weed,

But all I see is one too many a seed

Of hope,

Of love,

Dispersed in all directions of need.

———

DANDELION

Have you tried hugging a tree in spring?
You can almost feel the earth beat heart and soul
From the very core of its being.

It's like hugging life itself.

———

TREE HUGS

Yellow to green, the most beautiful transformation I've seen.

———

SPRING

Letting go of something you never had

Must be the easiest thing

...

Must be the hardest thing.

————

DIFFICULT

Rain through the windowpane…

Against the windshield like soft drumbeats, giving up life in the skies and sacrificing themselves like kamikazes willingly turning into stars against a backdrop of what is beyond.

———

DRIVING IN THE RAIN

If I often talk about clouds and rain, it's because there's just as much beauty in them as there is in sunshine…

It's all about perception.

Just don't label me as "sad" because I saw the sun shine in the dark.

———

WHERE THE SUN DON'T SHINE

You will have the urge to fix them, the desire to lift them up, the need to make them happy, and you will fail miserably—not because your love was not enough but because their love should be enough to fix themselves, to lift themselves up, and to make themselves happy.

Let them know you're there if they need you. They will come to you of their own volition.

———

ACCEPTANCE, PART I

I think in black and white.
  I feel in gray.
    //I love in multicolor.

———

KALEIDOSCOPE

;

céline zabad

Just the thought of you

        Makes my eyes squint.

———

ANATOMY OF A SMILE

He wanted me to stay in the moment with him

—

　　　　While it was fleeting,
　　While I was falling.

FALLING IN TIME

;

céline zabad

I stood between East and West

Thinking of you, forgetting the rest,
Because even between the two,
I was caught up in one,

Me and you.

———

0° 0' 0"

Salt and motion,

Like waves of an ocean,

Like tears of emotions.

———

HEALING

;

céline zabad

To leave you is to love where I am going enough to move on.

And I just can't do that.

———

AGONY

Our souls caught fire
    Before our eyes could meet. Who knew that
Our hearts could beat
    In such desire?
Now read from bottom to top…
    //When things mean what they mean.

————

WHAT YOU READ IS WHAT YOU GET

;

céline zabad

I only know how to give myself wholly,

completely,

utterly…

And maybe that gives you reason to think I take myself for granted.
And if I do, then it's only fair for you to do the same, because rare are
those who understand the intensity and immensity of giving one's all…

That it is neither an act of weakness nor a declaration of being easy.

———

ALL OF ME

We say we don't want to get attached to people because we don't know if they're temporary or not—

We forget that everything in this world is temporary, especially us.

———

MORTALS

Life is beautiful, but we weren't made for each other…

———

IRRECONCILABLE DIFFERENCES II

Do you want me for you or for me?
Because one is selfish and the other selfless...

———

ALL THE DIFFERENCE

Whoever thought that there should be a limit to giving?

//It's about to whom you choose to give.

———

GENEROSITY

When we lost you,
We lost all the men
We ought to know.

———

FATHER

She had no idea how to stop giving
until takers taught her how to…
//When takers are also givers.

————

THE LESSON

Sometimes you burn bridges only to become a bridge yourself.

Other times you're the bridge you have to burn.

———

ON BURNING BRIDGES

;

céline zabad

Stay with me in the moment,

In the present as we,

We become the past.

———

THE FUTURE

Like leaves of May
You move and sway,
As I get on a high
Of come what may:

Leave or stay.

AMSTERDAM

I can see right through you, and there's
nothing that terrifies you more.

———

TRANSLUCENT

Kiss me where it hurts the most,
            Where it's numb and cold—
As skin turns to gold and hearts melt and roast.

———

SUNSHINE

;

céline zabad

The night is young, so they say.
Toss and turn in the name of—
What keeps me up and takes my years away.

Pale all around, sickened by love,
Granting you my all,
Slowly dying in the skies above.

Loose strings hold me in thrall,
Chasing away all signs of sleep
As you rise and I—
I shall fall.

———

WHITE NIGHT

I cling on to ropes and hang in midair. A tear falls down, helplessly searching for a savior. Underneath is an empty space. No one to catch my falling tears—SPLISH. The shattering crash reverberates into my ears— SPLASH, the next kamikaze dives divinely into nothingness. Grace is gone, making way for pain. Underneath is an empty space.

ABYSS

;

céline zabad

In the late hours of the night,
I walk with a friend
Though miles away, never out of sight.

Keeping me company wherever I go,
Looking over me and letting me know,
Eyes above shine twinkle and glow,
For no one else but this friend below.

———

THE MOON

Of life and love,
On a windy day,
I wonder.

Of old ghosts,
Of wind,
Of light and dark,
Of lack of tears,
I fall.

———

WORDS ON A WINDY DAY

;

céline zabad

OUT OF TEARS…

And yet in my river I flow. I flow
To the sea,
Where I drown,
Sinking ever deeply.
I drown…

IN MY TEARS…

———

ORIGIN

And if I ever leave this world, know that it is not because it was too much for me to handle but rather because it couldn't handle all of me.

———

HEART

;

céline zabad

Where emotions are involved,
making sense of the senses is a lost cause.

———

NONSENSE AND SENSIBILITY

VOLUMES

So I got to thinking the other day, *What am I holding on to?*

You are no longer here, no longer physically with us, yet we carry the memory of you in our hearts and minds. It then occurred to me that a story unfolds when you flip the page. You move on even though the events are long gone and the characters no longer belong—you turn the page so that the story can continue, but in the end, you owe it all to the previous pages and all that they encompass. So although you're not here right now, you are still there, just on a previous page, a golden thread that adds to the beautiful tapestry of my story…and all those who have come and gone are also still there, just not here, right now on the current page I'm on…but it is those first pages, the previous ones that create the story, the very book of you.

———

PAGES OF A BOOK

;

céline zabad

How many times did our hearts and minds want to say something but chose not to—not only because "some things are better left unsaid" but because we could hear what the other was thinking, we were able to read between unwritten lines and words formulated in silence…We know, we just know. More often than not, silence sounds better, only because giving some words life could mean the death of something else: magic, unbridled thoughts and ideas, telepathic emotions in the making, you and me, us.

————

SILENCE

On a shore of what dreams may come,
My body lies willingly, giving in—
To the unremitting appeal to succumb,
Reluctantly—to the voices within.

Quench my thirst, rejuvenate my spirit,
Soothe my soul as it sinks ever more…
Into sand and sea, losing itself bit by bit,
Only to rise again and meet you at shore.

Take me away and in, with your ebb and flow.
Paint a silhouette of my alter ego.
Cool me down with the tip of your wave.
Give me a reason for my soul to save.

And all is well within a dream,
Hearts joined without a seam.
A pendulum of emotions, you come and go,
Leaving me fulfilled yet restless, to and fro.

Lost in passion and a sea of sin,
A reverie that could not have been.
"If I am a river, you are the ocean."
A pendulum together we put in motion.

Lash out at me with the whoosh of your flow,
A love once cherished in hopes to grow.
I strike back as you pull me in with your ebb…
Knotted and twisted, helplessly tangled in your web.

The moonlight searches for me in vain,
As I yearn for the dawn to break.
My heart has stopped; my soul's in pain.
What was is now a distant memory,
For I am fully awake…

———

AWAKENING

My soul lies deep within the earth,
But my spirit soars toward your light.
A heart of oak measured beyond its girth,
Standing tall and still with all its might.
With arms wide open, I call upon you,
Anxiously reaching out into the blue,
Awaiting the advent of a tear of bliss—
A droplet upon my side, a stolen kiss.
The springs of my life dance and sway
To the timid hymn of a gentle wind.
Waltzing graciously to the rhythm of the day,
Like the passionate liaison of bow and violin.
Song and dance, rhythm and beat—
All in an attempt to draw you in.
Surrender your love; bring forth your heat.
In us and this, my beloved, lies no sin.
Leaves and sheets of enchanting verse,
Swing back and forth to lift this curse.
As charm and grace anticipate the embrace,
Wind and leaf, both lost in space,
Yearn, ache, caress, and converse…
While I await the advent of a tear of bliss,
A droplet upon my side, a stolen kiss…

———

ODE TO THE HEAVENS

Take me back. Please do unwind,
Oh, dear hasty hands of time.
Give me back what once was mine;
Grant me a glance, a hint, or a sign.

Hold my hand, and guide me through
Long lost halls of me and you,
For I might stumble; I could fall
Upon what hangs on memory's wall.

Pictures and frames of light and shade
Reminding me of all that could naturally fade.
This path we built; those memories we made—
Bricks of tears and laughter on this road we laid.

This path seems naked, these halls so alone,
Save for cobwebs of a past that have been sewn.
Spiders of time crawl away from a dawn
That lies behind me, for ahead is a history foregone.

The light behind calls my name as I hold on
To shadows that know me more than the sun.
Summoning my soul to abandon what's done,
"Come back," it says. "Let bygones be bygone."

But you, old past, to me are dear.
Hold me close, and keep me near.
For you, my friend, hold the key
For all that I love and long to see.

Remnants of what the wind has left of you...
When did a one ever become a two?
Down memory lane I strut, with not a clue
Of when and where it all took place and for who,

As I question what still holds true:

Who am I, and where are you...

———

MEMORY LANE

Lost in time, staring into horizon's line,
Where sky and earth mingle and intertwine—
A lover's wish to be painted upon this dream,
Blending into the warmth of colors so serene.

Floating upon clouds of mystical reverie,
Putting to sleep all that is part of reality,
As the heavens reach out for a kiss
From all that is beneath and all that lives.

Like an innocent child embarrassed by the scene,
The sun heads down timidly toward its lair,
Blinking away yet revived by one-too-many a beam
As colors cold and warm mesh into a passionate affair.

As the sun blushes away and sets into the sea,
Promises of golden hue woo on bended knee,
Brides of tomorrow veiled in misty white,
Making way today for dancers of the night.

Dance tonight, oh, heaven and Earth,
And await at dawn the sun's rebirth.

King of summits is what you are,
Shining your light from afar,
Bursting with unfaltering emotion.
Dare you stand before such immaculate devotion?

For even an unwavering, fiery sun
Must slip away when the day is almost done.

From topmost heavens, you must come down,
Slowly and shyly bestowing your crown
To love unconditional; fade away thereof,
Leaving behind flames of a crimson love.

So, hopeless romantic, dream on into the sunset
As it opens the doors to lovers of the night.
Ponder upon your love and life with no regret.
Soon enough the sun will rise!

———

SUNSET UPON A KISS

I am but an autumn leaf
Dancing in midair,
Painting my way through the grief
Of colors that have left me bare.

I am but the wind,
Brushing against a skin,
Ruffling the locks
Of a love I feel within.

I am but the rain
Falling upon the earth,
Expressing the pain
Of a lack of worth,
Of a need for a rebirth.

I am but a stream
Flowing through life,
Attempting to create a blissful dream
Out of a reality filled with strife.

I am but the sky
Feeling lonely and blue,
Greeting clouds with a sigh,
Yearning for the light of stars so few.

I am but a lost soul
Wandering in space,
Searching for a goal,
Trying to find its place.

And if this you fail to see,
Then I have failed to be
What I wanted you to see:
The real me
In all that I am.

I am but what I am.
I am but me.
So take me as I am,
For I am what I am—
I am all this that is in me
And more.

I AM

I asked a dove
If it would bear my message,
If it could send my love
To a soul so precious.

I asked the wind
To carry words
Of a suffering heart
To those who are miles apart.

The dove and the wind
Failed to convey,
To their chagrin
And my dismay,

Tears of sorrow
That carried hopes of a tomorrow
And memories of a past
Struggling to last.

Wings of peace flap in vain,
But faith in the wind remains.
For my silence, it spread,
And my grief it shed.

Like a dandelion's seeds
Invisibly dressed in weeds,
I crumble in the air,
Disperse in despair,

Giving in to a soft kiss,
A tender caress,
A moment of bliss,
Short-lived happiness.

Fire to smoke,
Smoke in the wind,
I am no more
But silent words,
Waiting to be heard.

SILENT WORDS

Oh, with the advent of spring,
Does come many a wonderful thing.
The wind blows a tune so sweet,
Announcing the arrival of an uplifting beat.

The promise of tomorrow is born
As vim and vigor do adorn
Nature's face with colors that speak
Of budding roses upon her cheek.

Life is brought to life today
As grace and poise are put on display.
Never was beauty such defined
Or were its edges so refined

As this remarkable first day of spring,
Where even silence begins to sing,
And birds chirp while the storks do bring
The gift of love and life upon their wing.

You arrive with the advent of spring,
For with it—
Surely does come many a wonderful thing!

———

RIMA

REFLECTIONS

As we grow older, we tend to parent our parents and forget the years of wisdom they've put into making us who we are: adult children who think they always know best.

Take care of your parents, but do not confuse the roles.

———

SUNSET REFLECTIONS I

;
céline zabad

You can't control everything.
        Try not to control that as well.

//You are the only thing you can control.

———

SUNSET REFLECTIONS II

Chemistry doesn't have to do with the eyes and ears, lips and bodies, but everything to do with the lightning of minds, dancing of hearts—all in sync with souls older than time and more present than familiarity...

SUNSET REFLECTIONS III

;

céline zabad

He has a plan for you.
Trust it, no matter what your plan is.

———

SUNSET REFLECTIONS IV

Spirituality has nothing to do with religion; it has everything to do with faith.

Nurture that.

————

SUNSET REFLECTIONS V

Faith is what you practice with your heart.

Do not flaunt it; keep it where it belongs.
In your heart.

———

SUNSET REFLECTIONS VI

Blood is thicker than water, but both are
essential for life.

> Where the former swims through
> our veins, we choose whether to swim through
> the latter.

———

SUNSET REFLECTIONS VII

Do not force your children to follow a path you think is the right one, let alone the only one.

Show them; they will be more prone to choosing it if you let them make that decision.

————

SUNSET REFLECTIONS VIII

In due course—because the course was designed for you, with you in mind.

Be patient, for what is yours will be due. All in good time.

———

SUNSET REFLECTIONS IX

;
céline zabad

I know you love words.

Do not fall for them; listen to the tone of action behind them.
If they move you just as much, then by all means fall.

Fall hard.

———

SUNSET REFLECTIONS X

Time has a funny way of rekindling old relationships and molding a friendship that was barely even an acquaintance in the past—bringing together complete strangers who have barely crossed each other's path long ago.

Time has a funny way...
It has its reasons; trust it more often because it's simply beautiful...

———

SUNSET REFLECTIONS XI

;

céline zabad

Those who are gone are never really gone; all you have to do is listen and look carefully within.

They've been the beat to your heart ever since…

Listen…

———

SUNSET REFLECTIONS XII

"Sorry" goes a long way, but the shortcut is often more fulfilling:

Forgive, move on, and accept an apology that might never come...

———

SUNSET REFLECTIONS XIII

;

céline zabad

You might no longer be on speaking terms, but at a certain point in time, your exchanges spoke volumes of a loud conversation that reverberates even now.

They meant something then; they still do now and probably will in the future—even if you choose to deny it.

———

SUNSET REFLECTIONS XIV

Dysfunction is in every home; focus on the positive part of the word:
"Function."

———

SUNSET REFLECTIONS XV

And when you turn this page, question whether it was ink well spent…

The end.

———

THE AFTERMATH

About the Author

Céline Zabad wants to change the world, one word and insight at a time. Often characterized as "deep" by first impression and by those who know her well, Céline has been writing poetry since she was twelve. Her fans mostly praise her wit and distinct talent in translating complex feelings and relationships into sentiments that resonate with them personally, but Céline takes most pride being recognized by her digital followers for being able to listen and empathize across a virtual divide. She lends a courageous voice to many who feel paralyzed by emotion.

Born in Nigeria and raised in Lebanon, her upbringing and career have taken her across Africa, Europe, and the Middle East. When she isn't writing, Céline tries to balance her entrepreneurial spirit with her passion for people and social welfare.

From her soul to ink on white, to your heart her way she'll write…

See if Céline's words captivate you too.

https://www.instagram.com/celinezabad/

Made in United States
North Haven, CT
29 June 2023

38383607R30217